From Deep Within

AILSA CRAIG

BALBOA.
PRESS
A DIVISION OF HAY HOUSE

Balboa Press books may be ordered through booksellers or by contacting:

Balboa Press
A Division of Hay House
1663 Liberty Drive
Bloomington, IN 47403
www.balboapress.com.au
1 (877) 407-4847

Because of the dynamic nature of the Internet, any web addresses or
links contained in this book may have changed since publication and
may no longer be valid. The views expressed in this work are solely those
of the author and do not necessarily reflect the views of the publisher,
and the publisher hereby disclaims any responsibility for them.

The author of this book does not dispense medical advice or prescribe the use
of any technique as a form of treatment for physical, emotional, or medical
problems without the advice of a physician, either directly or indirectly. The
intent of the author is only to offer information of a general nature to help
you in your quest for emotional and spiritual well-being. In the event you use
any of the information in this book for yourself, which is your constitutional
right, the author and the publisher assume no responsibility for your actions.

Any people depicted in stock imagery provided by Thinkstock are models,
and such images are being used for illustrative purposes only.
Certain stock imagery © Thinkstock.

Print information available on the last page.

ISBN: 978-1-5043-1041-3 (sc)
ISBN: 978-1-5043-1040-6 (e)

Balboa Press rev. date: 09/21/2017

Dedication

Willow, Milla and Wyatt -
When you look at me, I see only love
When you smile at me, it's a gift from above

For my special friends Lynwen and Jenny who said, "I
think you should write a poetry book" – thank you.

I wouldn't have thought of it without your
support and encouragement.

Contents

Introduction

The book remains open
with pages to fill
from a place
found deep within my heart.
Words written with love
from experiences in life.
Moments of togetherness and
tears felt when our journeys
steered up apart.

ailsa craig

I have always loved writing poetry from a very early age. I found it was a way I could express how I felt as I found it difficult to communicate my feelings verbally, mainly due to shyness.

Different experiences in life; both personal and listening to others' stories and emotions, love, travel and moments spent in nature, have found their way out of deep within my soul, through the ink of my pen and onto the page.

I hope you enjoy my thoughts.

With love, Ailsa x

The night was perfect
for both the body and the soul.
The music that played
moved me to its tune.
Above the noise
of our physical world,
a silent voice spoke to me
through the veil of space.
"Hello," he whispered with his eyes.
I turned to see "him."
His eyes were a rich brown
that spoke volumes
as we met in the glance.
"Oh, hello," my eyes responded.
An immediate connection
was formed,
and we embraced each other with our smiles.
The language was silent
but loud.
We were the only ones
involved in this conversation
of intimacy and connection.
Our eyes and smiles danced
to our music,
experiencing sheer pleasure
together.
The more we connected,
the more intense our dance.
We needed no audible language
to understand our words.
Our music, our dance,
was beautiful.

When the time came
to go,
my eyes expressed sadness.
He answered with a smile.
My silent words cried,
"Please don't go."
He heard and blew me a kiss.
It was the nicest conversation
I have had for a while.
How I long for this
heart-to-heart
once more.

Life Is a Gift

The sun peeks through
cloud-filled curtains
as I open my eyes
to a new day.

Gentle rain falls
as it cleanses
my surrounds
and brings a sense of freshness.

Rise and greet the day
with a smile,
and appreciate that
we still breathe in the gift
of life.

Another day
to enjoy the view,
to hear the sounds,
to see the colours,
to feel the touch
of you.

Path of the Moon

Across the seas,
the moon provides
a path
for you to use.
Look beyond
what you can see,
beyond the golden hues.
And if you dare
to follow it,
by any means you will find.
The light
may become the reality
of that dream
that's never left
your mind.

Sunbeam

If I could catch
a sunbeam
and follow it
across the sea,
your face, your smile,
your everything,
is where I'd want
to be.

The lasting look
upon your face
has left me
with an empty space
in my life
and in my heart.
Why did we meet
only to part?

The Flight of the Bird

As you walk
in the morning light,
watch the birds
take off in flight.
Watch their grace
and wings of strength,
guiding them along
their journeys' length.
Become that bird;
look way below,
and try to find
that person whom you know
is the reason
you must go.

Don't be scared
to take that flight
through the darkness
into light.
Let go of fear
and soar above.
Find the place
where you feel love.

Looking Out My Window

Sometimes I get lost looking out my window.
My memories come flooding back
into my mind.
Oh, how I miss the days when I was
young.
With my friends on our adventures, we would find
places to hide, places to talk, places to be ourselves,
places where we could laugh and smile.
To each other, we were kind.
We had a pact.
We were very close
and, in fact,
best friends; those were the days.
Now we are aging, with children of our own.
Life's confusions, like being in a maze.
Trying to find a way to our dreams.
Life is a journey by whatever way,
by whatever means.

Looking out the window,
sometimes I shed a tear
that you are all so far away—
no longer close, no longer near.

The Rain

The rain comes down
so hard that I hear it on the roof.
It's nice inside.
The wet season is here.
We need no proof.
The sky is black.
I see no stars or moon
as beacons of light.
Just a steady fall of rain
in the darkness of the night.
Hold my hand, hold my heart,
hold my mind as distance
and darkness keep us apart.
I try to keep your eyes
in my memory strong.
As time and rain washes away
my feeling of you, O how I long
for you to always remain
in my heart and in my dreams.
But time has a way of taking away
anything good that has ever been.
My eyes still see
your eyes looking at me.
The rain can't take that away.
What will be will one day be.

Snatched Time

Sometimes
you listen
to a song
that takes you
to a place
in your space
in your memories.

Sometimes
you feel a touch
that means
so much,
or see a smile
that reminds you
once in a while
of the time
we drank
vodka and lime.
You looked
my way,
but the next day
took you
away.

And time
was no longer
our friend.

Waves of Thought

Sitting on the shore,
my toes buried in the sand,
I feel the tiny sharp
corners
of broken shells
nipping my skin.
The waves,
in continual motion,
lap the shore
and bring in treasures,
offerings from the ocean.
The wind is soft
and gentle
as it plays with my hair.
My thoughts
are far away.
I am in a peaceful place.
I am alone
but surrounded by
so much beauty.
Can you
remember me?
Can you
remember my smile?
I look out to sea.
You are so far away
but still so close
in my heart.

Moments Imprinted

To those
who have left
an imprint on my heart,
I hope that when you
look above and
see the clouds part,
you'll think about
times and moments
shared,
smiles and laughs, and
lasting looks from one
who cared.
My life was made
special.
You filled it with
a smile.
There are only a few
who leave their imprints,
and that just once in a while.

One Day

One beautiful day
when the sky is blue,
on a distant shore
I will find you.

And once again,
our eyes will meet,
a feeling so strong that
nothing can compete.

And once again
I will see your smile,
even though
it's been such a long while.

The time and days
that have kept us apart
will enhance our love,
your smile eternally
in my heart.

Time to Say Goodbye

I see the tear
in your eye.
I know it's hard
to say goodbye.

I watch you turn
on your heel,
trying so hard
not to show how you
feel.

And you walk towards
the open door,
both of us knowing in our hearts
that we wanted more.

The time we shared
was memorable,
full of stories and good times.
But now the end has come.
No more words to say.
No more rhymes.

"It's not you; it's me,"
we say.
But this time it is us.
We tried to see eternity.
Our tears will soon turn to dust.

Bringing You Back to Me

I want to write again.
I want to feel my words.
I want my words to dance
in your heart,
for you to feel my footsteps
gently exploring your soul.
In your soul,
I find a memory of our meeting,
a moment
when our eyes spoke
to each other
and an invisible thread of feeling
connected our hearts.
In my life, I have wondered
what such a moment
would feel like.
Because my days have
been hidden behind a mask—
a mask that covered many moments
of pure dread, fear, and loneliness.
Without that mask,
I could not have prevailed,
for it gave me a place to hide,
to pretend, to survive.
Then you looked over.
And I realised what I had
missed.

And then, just like that,
you left, turned, and blew me a kiss
that has stayed with me
in my heart.

It is all I was allowed—
a moment
in a distant country.
Two distant souls collided.
We spoke with different words,
but our eyes shared
the same language.
My mask has become
my norm now,
but my norm has two rooms.
One is filled with you,
a place I can escape to
and feel the veil of love
surround me for a while,
a secret place where I can
be again
and write poems to you,
bring you back to life,
back to me.

I want to write again.

Goodbye for Now

It's time to go, my love.
It's time to say goodbye.
I've tried to keep my tears at bay,
but it's so hard not to cry.
I think of all the days we've spent
together, just you and I.
It's hard now to imagine
my life will be just "I."
Thank you for the time we shared.
Together we got through.
I will love you for forever—
until the tides bring me to you.

Sometimes a cloud
can hide a sunbeam.
Sometimes a smile
can hide a tear.
Sometimes a silence
can hide a lost word.
Sometimes a word
can break your heart.
Sometimes a sunbeam
can give you life.
Sometimes a tear
can mean you are happy.
Sometimes silence
is overwhelming.
Sometimes a word
can be very special.
Sometimes we think
we make no difference.
But to the one who cares,
you can mean so much.

Reaching Out to You

Can I reach out
my hand
over tropical palms,
golden beaches, and
desert sand,
over oceans so deep
and lands far away,
over snow-capped mountains
and children at play?
Can I reach out
and touch you
and feel you so near?
In my heart is the
memory
of you I hold dear.

Your Eyes

I still see your eyes,
the nicest eyes I've seen
for a while.
I dived into their
serene pools
and followed the liquid
pathway to your
soul.
And there I found
home.

A Morning in Kokopo, Papua New Guinea

It was wonderful
sitting right up front on the bow
of our banana boat,
my legs dangling over either side.
We skimmed across the water's surface,
which was smooth like a mirror that day.
My toes tingled as the water splashed
up around me.
It was exhilarating.
The wind was playing with my hair
and tying knots in it with gay abandon.
Dolphins kept me company
and playfully splashed around
our boat.
As I tapped on the side, more came
and seemed to enjoy the company.
I know I did.
We headed for the swarm of seabirds
diving into the sea, trying to catch
a meal.
Huge tuna jumped out of the water
and teased us with their presence.
It was beautiful.
I was soaked
with a salty seawater film.
As we continued to bounce over
the surface of the sea,
up went my arms in absolute joy.

Remember this moment, I thought.
Nearby, locals in their canoes
waved and smiled.

Some had huge banana leaves
for protection from the sun.
I smiled; it made sense but looked funny.

The volcano gave the occasional puff
we were used to observing,
hoping that's all it would be.

What a day in paradise.

Can't Complain

I was thinking about things—
you know, the usual stuff—
about life and memories
that sometimes make you tough.
I was lucky to have a great family
and friends. I still have many.
I've travelled to lots of nations
and spent more than just a penny.
I really can't complain that much.
Just sometimes life gets me down.
I find it hard not to smile,
and I hate things that make me frown.
I've shared many a love story
with some wonderful men in tow.
I remember their lovely faces,
and the sadness when it was time to go.
I've also suffered mental abuse
and shed many a tear at night,
lying in my bed and wondering,
How did I start that fight?
My children are my everything,
my light, my shining stars.
I cannot complain about anything,
and I've learnt to hide my scars.

So, as I lie here thinking
And life keeps moving on,
I know I have been lucky
With all who share my song.

Missing You

I miss playing
the piano,
something I
loved
to do,
especially
the music
that came to me
while I was
thinking
of you.

My Journey

And off I go
on a journey
to a place
I've yet to see,
where my heart
will find
what it's missing
instead of what
it remembers
from a memory.
Along the path
I'll wander
and look forward
to what lies ahead,
and hope it all—
the confusion,
the path—is clear
of uncertainties
and leads to
a home for my heart
instead.
And if my journey
does stop here
and all I have
dreamt about is real,
my life will be
more than happy.
Of that I am sure.
I will feel.

With wind in her mane,
she dances through
the turquoise seas
of the Scottish shores
and blends into the purple
heather hues of
the mystical highlands.
Her majesty
is wild and free.
Her strength
is pure and true.
Her home is a magical
mist
where stories are born
and legends are created.
It is a place to believe in
what you dare to dream—
if you let her magic
take you there.

Winter

The wind bites
right through me.
I feel its grip
get tighter
and tighter
as it surrounds me.
The droplets
of moisture in the air
cut my skin
like broken
shards of ice.
The trees bow
with the weight
of snow
on their branches
as my boots
crunch through
the carpet of ice and snow
that lies before me.
The sky is as blue
as I have ever seen it.
The light of the sun
tells me it's daytime.
Any warmth provided
is overtaken
by the extreme coldness
of winter.
But I feel alive.
My senses are awakened
as they dance
to the tune
of falling temperatures
and exhilarate
in its freshness.

My Soldier

I have a soldier
in my heart.
The distance
between us
keeps us apart.
He fought in battles
unbeknown to me.
I'm sure his courage
set many free.
I don't know
where my soldier
roams,
for we live in
different homes.
I blow a kiss
into the breeze.
I whisper messages
across the seas.
Maybe one dawn
I will find him near.
Until then,
in my heart, I know
he's here.

A New Day

The sun filters through
the curtains
and gently touches
my cheek
like a warm touch
of yesteryear.
The distant buzz
of a plane sounds
as it merges into
the pink and blue smudge
of the afternoon sky.
The birds start
their morning chorus
as the dogs' tails
are wagging
at the thought
of a walk.
It's another day
to open up and
see what's inside.

Little Man

I see your gentle spirit
shining each time
you smile,
a smile that warms
a cold day in winter.
You make the stars
appear at night
and add such sparkle
to our world.
Your eyes are as blue
as the sky above
and as deep as the seas
of our emotions.
Your heart is our island
escape,
when sadness is in
the air.

A gift under the
tree of life.
A gift to all who touch
the light of your
sweet soul.

The Pond

It's a beautiful pond
by which I sit.
Just a few gentle ripples
form wrinkles on its surface.
The hue of the water
is very blue,
trying to match
the summer sky.
The green reeds stand tall with
their feet in the water,
enjoying the view.
The shades of green against the blue
elicit an emotion
I find hard to describe.
Nature's artistic excellence.
There is a warm glow from the sun
adding sparkle
to the surface of the pond.
Such a peaceful place to sit
and collect my thoughts
as I disappear into the depths
that lie before me.
In my mind
I dive into the cerulean
with a sense of the sublime,
another world
full of life busily going about its day.
I feel the peace
in my mind
floating calmly in my spiritual place
of bliss,
observing without cause

to fear.
As I head for the light,
filtering and dispersing the colours
of this foreign land,
slowly I awake
and melt into the soft green grass
of my surrounds.

Morning at the Beach

The beach is beautiful today.
The morning air is losing its crispness
as the sun slowly rises from the horizon.
The sun stretches its rays
out in all directions
and warms me with its glow.
The waves gently kiss the shore.
My toes tingle as the waves
surround me and I sink into the wet sand.
I dive into the clear waters
and feel a freshness and exhilaration
sweep over me.
The sunlight penetrates the watery layers
and lights up small treasures
dotted along the sea floor.
I reach down and pick up a shell.
It's cracked and a bit rough
around the edges
but still amazing in its structure.
We are like the shell,
signs of life's struggles imprinted
on our body and soul.
As I leave the cleansing blue waters
of the sea,
my footprints are swallowed up by
each incoming wave;
my presence is melted away.
More people arrive.
Their smiles ignite my heart.
As I breathe in deep, the salty air
fills my being.
It's invigorating.
I'm ready to start the day.

The Lone Piper

The lone piper stands atop
an ancient wall.
The haunting sounds
of the bagpipe
fill the lochs and burns
that surround him.
The mountains listen
in awe.
The sounds clench my soul
with a fistful of feeling.
My eyes fill with tears.
My heart fills with love.
My blood turns the colour
of the heather,
painting the hills in purple.
And I feel free
yet very connected
to the lovely sounds and the beauty
that has entranced me.

Darkness falls.
The remnants of the sunset have dissolved into
the night sky.
The sounds of daily life are
different and quieter.
There is the odd bark from a dog, and laughter
from a nearby gathering.
I look up at the moon.
Her beaming face smiles
down at me.
"It's OK," she whispers. "He will come. He is
following the path of light I laid out for him.
One day you will meet again and your smile
will return."
The sound of a distant siren breaks the
mesmerising gaze I have with the moon.
You are right, I think.
*One day I will turn around
and he will be there.*

Can You?

Can you walk with me
so I don't lose my way?
Can you talk with me
so I don't lose my voice?
Can I look at you through my eyes
so I don't lose my sight?
Can I give you my love
so I don't lose my heart?

Can I hold your hand
so I can enjoy your touch?
Can you look at me and smile
so I know you see me?
Can you kiss me with a gentle passion
so my senses awaken?
Can I stop asking questions
and know your answers are all that I seek?

Trying to Let Go

Wherever you are,
I hope you are safe.
Whatever you are doing,
I hope it brings you joy.
Whomever you are with,
I hope they surround you with love.
Whatever you remember of me
doesn't matter,
because you have left
a footprint on my heart,
along with others
who have passed by.
You gave me a gift
that was so special to me.
I'm just glad that
where you were then
was where I happened to be,
and that that place
was ours.

À la prochaine (Until next time)

Beautiful Paris,
it's been a few years
between visits.
The first time I met you,
I was a young adventurer
pining for a story.
You didn't seem so big.
I found my way around you
very easily.
It rained every day I was
with you.
It didn't stop me from exploring
your beauty, your architecture, or from
standing under the Eiffel Tower
and feeling amazing.
"I'm here," I whispered.
I bought a navy-blue beret
and a pair of tan ankle boots.
I was in awe of the Parisian style,
the fashion, the cafés, the coffee,
the people, the little apartments
with flowers adorning
their windows.
It would be a long time
before I saw you again
and experienced the lure of your soul.
The City of Love.
I felt so lost
this time.
So many trains and crowded
carriages, gendarmes, and sirens.
But still the style that I love

remained,
the language, the food,
the avenue des Champs-Élysées.
You still have my heart.

Paris, je t'aime.
Au revoir.

Don't Leave

I try to clear my mind
to think of thoughts
that will take me
away,
but I know
you are fading.
I can't sense you
as much.
I used to know
when you were with
me.
Even though you are
a million miles away,
you are the
inspiration for my
words.
You brought my soul back to life,
but you are fading.
Life is taking you
away from me.
Please hold on
if you can.
The horizon is as far
or as close as your
mind wants it to be.

New Life

Your tiny hand, so
beautiful to hold.
Skin so soft and new.
Your little features
will fill out in time
to reveal the real you.
How amazing that
you are here. Your
journey has just
begun.
Your life will be filled
with many things. I
hope it's lots of fun.
I wonder who you are
inside, who looks out
through your eyes.
That's what makes
life wonderful. You are
a gift, a beautiful
surprise.

Photographs and Memories

Sometimes it's nice
to stop awhile
and browse through moments
now gone.
I see faces of friends with smiles
so nice,
and I hear laughs we shared for
so long.
I look at places we visited
and loved either briefly or stopped at
for a while.
I smile with fondness for the memories.
Shared friendships added to life's
file.
Time goes by. We walk
a different track,
but it's still nice to remember
and let our thoughts enjoy
going back.

Good Night

The wind swirls around me,
gently picks me up,
and carries me
along its guided path.
I feel its soft breath
surround me
as it provides a cradle
in which I lie.
I look down and see my life
full of hope, dreams, losses,
tears, laughter, children,
desires.
I look behind me
and see all I have left
slowly disappearing
into nothingness.
I try to look beyond,
but it's too misty
to see.
I try to blow the mist away,
but it engulfs me.
I cannot see,
but I can feel
a feeling of great contentment
and calm.
A familiar hand stretches
through the mist.
'Is it you?' I ask softly.
There is no reply,
just a feeling of pure joy.
I am home.
I shut my eyes.

I feel safe within the wind.
With the familiar hand wrapped gently around mine,
into sleep I go,
knowing you are forever
with me.

You and She

Can you see the look
in her eyes
when she looks your way?

Can you see the smile
on his face?
I think you just made his day.

Can you feel his hand
on your shoulder,
gentle but full of care?

Can you see how lovely
she glows
just knowing you are there?

Can you feel the touch
of her hand
as she lets you know she's near?

Can you see how loved
she feels
when you whisper sweet words
in her ear?

Can you feel the emotion
she has
when she remembers the day

you just happened to be
in the same room as her
and decided to look
her way?

Himalaya

Your mountains, so beautiful,
so majestic.
They stand tall
like a guard of honour,
way above the clouds.
They stretch like a pathway
to heaven.
Your beauty is unmatched
as I stare in absolute wonder
and bathe
in the never-ending glory
of your majesty.
So many have walked
the path we follow.
So many have gazed endlessly
at your panoramic magic.
You haunt my memories,
my heart,
my desire to once again
feel the power
you have over our souls.

One Sign, One Word

I do not know
where you are.
I search for you
constantly.
I yearn to see
your face once more.
Your eyes are burnt
into my soul.
Why don't you
write?
It was you
who hooked
my heart
with your smile,
and now
you are silent.
Your world is
so far from mine,
so different.
It made you
who you are,
so I embrace it.
One word
is all I need
to know
you have not left me.
One word.

A Letter to My Mother

Dear Mum,

There are times when I sit and ponder
memories along my path.
I can see your loving smile
and hear your classic laugh.
I remember all the stories
we'd share of times gone by,
or the long conversations
that would sometimes make us cry.
Life just keeps on rolling.
We no longer sit and talk.
Your passing has left a gap in my life,
like cutlery without a fork.
But I can still hear your laugh
when I stop and think
and hear our conversations
around the kitchen sink.
And when my time comes
to join you in that place,
we will catch up on all our stories
and fill that empty space.

A Letter to You

My dear love,
you are the calm sea
of my soul.
You are all I breathe
from day to night.
You inspire my poetry,
which flows through my pen.
Your smile has
never left my heart.
Your eyes have
never left my sight.
I cannot stand the thought
of never knowing you,
of never surrounding you
with the love I feel.
Why did life
separate our hearts
and prevent them from
becoming one?

A Special Place

There is a place
I sometimes go.
Maybe it's somewhere
you might know.
Beyond the realms of all
that is real,
a place to dance, to write,
to feel.
It's full of mountains and
oceans so deep,
and all the memories
I've been allowed to keep.
I dance through the daisies
that fill my path.
I skip through blue waters,
watch bears have a bath.
The night sky is so clear;
the stars are so bright.
I lie in the grass
and stare in delight.
There are no tears here.
No place for remorse,
it's a place to feel peaceful—
and happy of course.
I'd like to share
my special place with you,
but you need to be
unashamedly *true*.

Memories
clouding my thoughts.
A continual slide show
of a smile, a kiss,
the touch of your skin,
the feeling of bliss
and longing.
I sense the soft feel
of your shaved cheek
and see the tinge of grey
in your hair.
I see the deepness in your eyes
just looking at me,
and I just want to wrap
myself around you
and never let you go.
I feel your presence
in my thoughts so strongly that
sometimes
I whisper, "Hello."
The slide show ends
as I leave the world
my memories sometimes take me to
and as my mind returns
to focus on reality.

Playing with Waves

The waves engulf me.
They toss me around like a rag doll.
I try to fight through
the boiling, bubbling white foam.
The force of the waves
pushes me down farther as I battle
against their strength.
The sea has me in its grip.
I can't breathe.
I try to focus my eyes.
The sun puts on a show of dancing light
in green and blue
as it filters through
this watery mass.
I can't give in.
A calmness comes over me.
I slowly surface and breathe.
I love this world.
It takes me on a ride
I fear and accept,
then gently carries me back
and places me on the sand
like a wounded soldier
it respects.
I catch my breath
and lie still in the
shallows as the waves
carefully tend to my
hidden wounds.

My Tears

You do not understand the
words my tears speak.
You do not understand
the coldness in your tone
and how it breaks my heart.
You do not understand
that the look in your eyes
does not speak
love.
You do not understand
me.

Always with Me

While there are still stars
in the sky
and the sun
to warm our day;
while there's still rain
to make puddles
in which children play;
while there are still people
with smiles
to warm up your heart,
or tears that are shed
when you know
you must part;
while flowers still bloom
and I can hear your kind
voice,
I know you are here
with me,
and that is
your choice.

Moonlight Dance

Slow dancing
in the moonlight,
round and round.
My hair tickles my cheek
as it plays with my shoulders.
The gentle kiss of the night
seduces my senses.
I love the music.
The notes are like beautiful words
whispered in my ears.
Your breath is close.
It's warm and soft as it gently touches
my skin.
Your hand finds its way into mine
as I rest my head against
your chest.
Slow dancing
with you.

Clan Gordon

The tartans fly and colour the sky.
The sound of the bagpipes
fills the valleys.
The hills we climb
bear the strength
of our hearts.
The bridges we cross
are monuments to our
victories.
Our clans are one
with many.
Our colours are true
and strong.
We fight for our dignity
and soldiers' courage.
Our blood stains
the rivers of our souls.
The stag watches,
strong and steadfast.
He will only flee
when hope is lost
and his sanctuary
is no more.

Are You Still Mine?

What makes a smile
last more than one night?
What makes a look
remain within my sight?
What would make you stay?
Or if I turned,
would you let me walk away?
If your fingers
could caress my face
with a sweet and tender touch,
would you see the look
in my loving eyes
trying to express so much?
Would you hear my heart
quicken
as you gently took my hand
and catch my look filled with shyness,
or would your thoughts return
to your distant land?
Do you ever think
about that night
our eyes were locked
in time?
Or have you shared
that gaze with another
and I have lost
that which for a moment
was mine?

Beyond the Sea

When you look out to sea,
can you feel the serenity
or feel the life
that surrounds your senses?
A sense of freedom.
I see no fences.
A calmness as the waves do slumber.
For many a journey, they encumber,
carrying ships from port to port,
providing pleasure in the sense of sport.
The winds start blowing
and bring a sense of fear.
Dark clouds gather
over seas so near.
I must away and find a place
where my senses feel safe
within this space.

Sunset of My Day

The sun slowly melts
into the far horizon.
All the shades of orange
and pink
light up the sky
with such beauty
like a last hurrah
before darkness takes over.
A slight breeze
gently blows my hair.
I lean back and close my eyes,
surrounded by silence.
It's so peaceful
sitting here, eyes shut,
feeling the dampness of the grass
seeping through the layers of my clothes.
There is music in this silence
performed by nature,
a choir of natural sounds
softly playing in my ears.
I am alone here.
The darkness engulfs all I can see.
No moon tonight, just stars
twinkling above,
thousands of stars to wish upon.
The cold touches my skin
and I shiver.
It's time to go, time to leave my
bliss,
to venture into the darkness,
to find light, to find home.

Flames of Delight

Sitting beside the fire at night,
watching the flames play
with such delight.
A glass of red.
I've had a couple,
making me believe
I am quite supple.
You take my hand
and hold me tight.
This has been such
an enchanted night.
I can't remember
when I've felt so fine.
Is it possible
you could be mine?
The sparks from the fire
crackle and pop
as you wrap me in your jumper.
I feel quite cool on top.
I see you smiling,
staring at the fire.
I love this picture,
and you, I so admire.
As we toast to our life,
a gentle kiss is bliss to my heart.
The trees close in around us.
Do we really have to part?
Can I tell you how much
this night fills me with love?
A night 'round the fire
with magic, a gift from above.

Rain on My Window

It's raining outside my window.
Soft gentle droplets cover the glass
and blur my view of the outside.
The constant tapping on the roof
is quite comforting.
I'm rolled up in a ball on the couch.
My glasses are becoming more of a
fixture as I do more writing.
They tilt and drop, trying to find a spot on which to rest,
aiding my vision, giving me a sharper perspective on life.
As I write, my mind wanders, trying to lead me away from my
present moment.
I try to come back, try to focus,
but off I go to visit people, places,
and imagination.
The rain stops. There's a glistening of light as the sun filters
through the thick layer of glass in the window frame.
Glasses off, I stretch out the full length of the couch.
Eyes shut, I go back into the world of my thoughts.

Never Forget

There's an echo in the breeze;
it's calling out her name.
Listen very carefully.
There it goes again …
It's very soft and distant,
as if from somewhere far.
She looks up to the heavens.
Could it be from a distant star?
The breeze swirls around her;
it has a warm and gentle touch.
She feels a kiss upon her cheek.
"Is it you I sense so much?"
The voice she can hear—
very faint, but still it's there.
"Do you know I'm thinking about you? For so long. I still do
care."
She places her hand upon her heart
and looks to the sky above.
"Please never forget me," she sends upon the breeze.
"Never forget my love."

Look Beyond

Look beyond the trees;
come take a peek.
Separate the branches.
Be quiet; do not speak.
Take a step forward.
Can you see the yellow glow?
It's a special place—it's magic—
where only we can go.
When we go beyond the trees,
there's no turning back.
We follow the yellow brick road.
Imagination, we do not lack.
The road will take us far
away into our dreams.
For what lies beyond the trees
is exactly as it seems.
Are you ready to take the step
into the magic city of ours,
which is past the deepest oceans,
forests, mountains, and stars?
You will feel the magic
surround you.
It will light up the skies.
And you'll know how much you mean to me
when you look into my eyes.

Our Magical New Day

When the light of a new day calls you,
I'll be ready when you awake.
My magic carpet awaits you;
new places we will go, new adventures we will take.
We'll fly towards the sunrise,
soak in all the colours of dawn.
A new day is beginning;
never again will you feel forlorn.
We'll visit many places;
new people we will meet.
A new day is beginning;
you're safe on my magic carpet seat.
Try not to look down
if you think that you will fall.
Just focus on what lies ahead.
Can you hear the mountains call?
I want to take you with me
wherever I may roam.
Together we are such a bright light.
Together we are home.

Cool Satisfaction

And in I go,
sinking into the cool water
that surrounds me.
Down deep I dive,
beautiful, refreshing.
I let my body
float in harmony
with the gentle ripples
that lick my limbs
with a subtle coolness.
As I close my eyes,
I feel a calmness and serenity
in this watery world
that tries to satisfy
my desires.

Dance of Seduction

Can you feel my soft breath
as I whisper in your ear,
"Wake up"?
Can you feel the heat from my body
as I move closer into your space?
Can you smell my seductive perfume
as it surrounds your sleeping soul?
Can you feel my fingertips
as I softly touch your face?
Can you feel my warm lips
as they gently caress your body?
Can you feel my tingling hands
as they try to bring you pleasure?
Can you feel my beating heart
as it quickens with delight?
Can you feel me?

The Seed

A tear from the moon
fell heavily on her heart
until she realised it was a gift
and decided to part …
She followed a path
and wondered where it would lead.
The tear that had fallen
merely planted the seed.
It's up to you to ease your heart's pain.
When you can move forward,
you have so much to gain.

Seasons

Each step through autumn leaves
scattered here and there, and
each step through fresh white snow,
awakens my senses. And
each step through the beautiful blossoms
adorning my path,
each step through ocean waters,
cools my body. And
each step through the seasons
leads me closer
to you.

When You Look at Me

Can you see me across the table?
I'm the one with eyes of blue.
Can you see how I don't look away?
I can't bear not to look at you.
Can you see the desire in my eyes
when I capture your glance?
Can you see how I long for you
to ask me for a dance?

Can you see the blush upon my cheeks
when you look my way?
Can you hear me when I giggle
with thoughts of us at play?
Will you listen to my words of passion
when you hold me in your arms?
Will you hear my pleas for more
as you saturate me with your charms?

Do you know how much you mean to me,
that I've never felt this way?
Do you know that when I look at you,
night turns into day?
Do you know the smile you gave me
took me by surprise?
Do you know what happens within me
when you look into my eyes?

A Walk in Nature

Nature takes me by the hand
as I wander into the forest
surrounded by trees, by wild flowers, by beauty.
The leaves whisper as they rustle in the breeze.
Nature's melody.
A leaf falls
slowly,
touching me gently on the cheek
as it floats by.
Something is moving.
Eyes,
eyes everywhere.
Who is the stranger in our midst?
Smells.
Smells of moistened earth and leaves.
There's misty rain in the air,
dampening all it can touch.
Freshness
as I breathe in the natural aromas
that fill the air.
Raindrops gently land,
slowly rolling down my nose and
then jumping off the tip with gay abandon.
Sounds
as I reach an opening in this quiet world.
I hear a different sound:
waves
gently making their way to shore.
Before me lies a sea of turquoise,
another natural wonderland.
Different smells.
Different touches to feel.
Same senses:
serenity, peace, acceptance, love.

Floating on a Chant

It's morning.
The grass is very soft to sit upon.
There are lots of tiny perfectly formed
balls of dew
resting precariously on each blade of grass.
I close my eyes
and face towards the rising sun.
I can feel the warmth of her rays
close around me
like a hug filled with love.
The background chant of a CD
I bought in Nepal
carries me away.
I float on the notes
over the seas,
back to the mountains of Himalaya
and the streets of Kathmandu.
The chant takes me back down
the little winding roads
filled with colour and noise.
The air is imbued with incense and spices.
I see the smiles on the worn, tired faces
of the Nepalese,
always carrying a smile in their pocket.
I love the way I feel,
but I have to return
on the notes that carried me back
to my memories.
They carry me back home.
As I open my eyes,
I feel a sense of calm.
As the melodic chanting ceases,
I am ready to face the day.

Are You Here?

Who are you?
Where are you?
I've been waiting for you …
Or will you appear in the next life?
I loved our life together.
Am I not good enough in this life?
It's lunchtime on my life clock.
I've enjoyed many entrées,
As I'm sure you have.
Maybe I'll skip the main course and just enjoy dessert.
Are you here in this present world?
Do I know you?
Or is it all a figment of my life's imagination,
a need to fill an empty seat?
Or is it nature trying to complete
a two-piece jigsaw puzzle?
Ah, who cares?
I hope our path in the next life is easier,
that we can enjoy a laugh or two,
and that we remember our sparkle.
I'll see you then …
Look for me.
I can't wait to see you
again.

A memory.
A photo.
A heart
broken.

A tear.
A sigh.
A word left
unspoken.

A wish.
A desire.
A look to the
horizon.

A memory.
A sad heart
left
unopened.

My Faraway Love

Blow ye, breeze,
with flowers adorned.
Take me with you
o'er seas forlorn.
For if my love
dost wait for me,
I will remain
in heavenly
desire
to lay my eyes
upon his face.
Then I'll know
I've found my place
where my heart
remains true.
From where I lie,
my eyes are on you.
So take me, breeze;
take my hand
and lead me to
this faraway land.
And once you know
your job is done,
there you'll
leave me,
and my new life will
have begun.

Postcard from Plockton

It was misty the day we drove
from Kyle of Lochalsh to the cabins
just outside of Plockton.
Our trio of cars
flowed along the small dirt road
as it wove its path through cosy villages
nestled in the hills beside Loch Alsh,
over little bridges, past highland cattle,
until the turn-off into the forest.
It was here amongst the trees
that we found our little log cabins.
Armed with hot fish and chips from
picturesque Plockton,
we snuggled in for the night.
The air here was full of chilly freshness
that nipped our cheeks
and made our breath visible
as we spoke.
The surrounding bush was green and moist,
and full of flowers
wearing all sorts of colours and styles.
The sound of the creek
behind the cabins
played such a beautiful melody
as it made its way over rocks and logs
that lined its path.
Our home for the next few days was
beautiful.

Photo of You

I opened up the page again,
the one I left behind.
I thought I'd put you in my memories.
I knew you'd be too hard to find.

But when I looked at your photo,
your eyes looked straight into mine,
like you had come alive again,
like going back in time.

I could feel your cheek so close,
your lips just a breath away.
Your smile still sits upon my heart—
a gift you gave to me that day.

There's such a strong sense I have of you.
I still feel your presence so near,
even though the past years
have left me
forever wanting you, my dear.

Do I turn the page again
and try to look upon you no more,
the photo and the memory
like a faded footprint upon the floor?

Blank Pages

My mind has gone blank.
I feel like an empty page
longing for words
to decorate my lines.
Maybe it's the heat.
Maybe it has wearied the thoughts
that usually flow.
Maybe it's the emptiness
I feel in my soul,
feeling so distant
from all those I love.
Maybe it's time,
time to take the next turn-off
and see where it leads.
The page just stares at me.
No more cries from a love long gone.
There's no solace in writing words
filled with tears.
It only brings sadness.
The page should be filled
with smiles and colour.
Who knows?
Maybe at the next turn,
the signpost will read,
To the Unknown.
This path will light my way
and take me to a new page.
My pen will flow again
like a river after the rain.
And life will be given another chance
as it drinks from nature's cup.
The flowers will bloom again.

And the words I write
will be full of new meanings,
new adventures, new beginnings.
Yes, this is what I hope for.
This page will remain blank
until it can be filled with a spark
that ignites a feeling
of passion, of joy,
endearing its readers
to the possibility
that endings can be happy
and that life is indeed
precious and sweet.

Memories of Home

I felt a deep sadness
as I wandered up the path
to the front door.
The path was how I remembered it,
broken and cracked, like a trap for an
unsuspecting visitor to trip on.
The garden was still the same,
just a bit more overgrown.
I could hear the faint voices
of my childhood,
laughing and giggling
with my sisters and friends.
The hydrangea bush
still adorned the lounge room window.
I have always loved hydrangeas
because of this;
they make me feel at home.
I remember cold winter days
walking up this path,
with the smell of the open fire
drifting up the chimney into the air.
The fire warmed the whole house
and was so cosy to sit around.
The children's voices
turned into teenage chatter.
I recall boyfriends
holding my hand
as they escorted me to the front door.
Then the kiss good-bye,
so tender, so sweet.
I remember the parties, the music,
the whispers, the "glad to be home"

feeling after school,
the relatives, the best friends, the strangers,
all those who walked along this path.
I can hear our dogs barking,
our budgies chirping, our children laughing,
the piano playing, so much music in the air.
So many memories!
As I reach the front door,
I know it will be the last time.
I turn the doorknob.
The house has been sold.
Mum and Dad are together
in another realm.
All our memories have been packed up.
All that remains is an empty shell
of so many years of our family life.
The house is to be demolished
along with all our dreams, laughter, sadness, and love, and
our life as us.

Teardrop

It was the look
she never saw coming.

It was the smile
that melted her heart.

It was the gentle way
he said goodbye.

It was the tear
that forever remained.

The Performance

It's hot.
The air is thick with humidity
as the clouds gather en masse.
The show is about to start,
a seasonal performance of *Storm*.
There will be a thrilling light show
as the rich loud voice of thunder
is heard above the choir of rain.
As it pelts out its tune,
I watch the performance
from my shelter in the forest
under the huge leaves of
the banana palm,
which bend with the weight
of the rain's song,
covering me with its damp notes.
I then tiptoe
from one stepping stone to another,
a bridge over the fast-filling clear water creek
to the other side.
A sharp crack shoots a bright ray nearby
that lights up the area around me.
Then darkness returns
as thunder sings
with a loud voice
and the rain tries hard
to keep in tune.
The show goes on for some time.
The level of the creek has risen
and covers my stepping-stone bridge.
The clouds then start to separate
and go their own way.

Thunder's voice is quietening
and the light show is over.
The performance was memorable.
Time to head out of the darkness,
find my sodden track that leads
to my destination—dry, cool comfort.

Is It You?

Is it your light I see
that appears in the night?
Is it your voice I hear
calling me?
Confused,
I try to clear my mind,
but it is like a Scrabble board.
And with each letter I pick,
I try to write another name,
but it always spells yours.
Do I allow myself
to follow this light?
Do I allow myself
to answer your call?
Is it my imagination
that is playing with my heart?
Or is it truly you?
Should I let you go
or let distance keep us apart?
Shyness is my enemy.
Confidence always comes in
second.
Is it in your arms
I will feel your beautiful heart
surround me with a love so pure
that it gives my heart
a home?

My Wish

Sometimes I wish upon a star.
I close my eyes
and see far
away in my dreams
a cottage, a beach,
much more than it seems,
a place so nice,
and you standing there
warm and handsome,
adding spice.

The star shines bright
and gives me a wink.
I hope it knows something.
What do you think?
I smile and hope my wish
is real,
because I know
what my heart does feel.

I Feel You

Mist seeps over the horizon,
covering the bay as it moves
closer to shore.
The wind whispers through
the trees,
bringing
voices from the past.
Rustling the leaves as they pass by,
they gently let me know
they are there,
softly kissing my cheek
and playfully mussing
my hair.
I close my eyes.
The mist envelops me.
For a moment
I feel you, I hear you.
You are with me.

To Just Be

Is it too late
to follow the seabird
as it flies into the sun?

Is it too late
to let the waves
carry me into oblivion?

Is it too late
to ride a blue whale
as it swims through the deepest oceans?

Is it too late
to just enjoy the sunset
and listen to the song of the sea?

Is it too late
to just be?

To Dance

When I listen to music
and dance,
all the worries of the world
are far away from me.

When I listen to music
and dance,
I close my eyes and let the music
of the rhythm enchant me.

When I listen to music
and dance,
I feel alive and let the feeling
set me free.

My Friend

Sometimes in life,
someone will come along
and sit beside you.
You may see this person
every day, once in a while, or for just
a moment in time.
You will always remember them
for their smile, their words, their way—
because they have touched your soul
in a way that only a few can.
They are your friend.
And your heart keeps only those
it knows
it can hold onto and cherish,
those who will never leave.

Is It Wrong?

Is it wrong
to want to smile,
to smile so big
that it stretches your cheeks?
Is it wrong
to want to feel this smile
melt your insides,
so much so that you want to tell the world?
Is it wrong
to want to feel so strongly
that you can only dance with delight?
Is it wrong
to want someone
who adores your company
so much
that no words are needed,
just a beautiful silence
of two hearts connecting?
It is wrong
when you're all wrung out
to want to feel alive again,
to jump or walk
with a spring in your step,
because you know
someone will catch you and hold you
should you fall?
Is it so wrong
after so much giving
to enjoy receiving the gift
of a genuine smile and heart?
Is it wrong
to enjoy the company of a friend
when you just need to feel
special?

The Tree by the Sea

Can you see me standing here?
My branches are waving in the breeze
that swirls all around me
as I stand on guard by the seas.
What do you see
when you look at me?
Am I a thing of beauty
or just simply a tree?
You can sit beneath my foliage
and seek shelter from the sun.
Some may swing on or climb my branches,
finding ways to use me for fun.
As the seasons come and go,
I stand here all alone.
I watch the moods of the ocean;
it depends on the winds to set the water's tone.
I've had waves crash around me,
calm waters gently lap the sand.
I've had many strangers sit beneath me.
My life as a tree here will never be bland.

You Are Here

The light from the moon
seeped through the thin veil
of my curtains.
A cool breeze entered my room
and slowly encircled me,
caressing every inch of my body,
softly, gently
sweeping my tangled hair off my face
and tickling my neck
with a touch of warmth
as it swirled playfully around me.
My cheek tingled with delight
as the breeze lightly kissed it and
then whispered, "Hush now," into my ear.
I looked towards the window
and watched the curtains dance
in the breeze,
yet the window remained shut.
No shadows lurked in the light of the moon,
but I wasn't alone.
The wind chimes played a beautiful melody
as I felt my senses float into ecstasy.
"I feel you," I whispered, smiling and then closing my eyes.
"You have never left me.
Our souls are one."
As I dive into the tranquil waters of sleep, I feel such peace.
I know that as I sleep through each night
and as I walk through each day,
I am never alone.
You will always be with me, through each lifetime, together.
We will always find each other,
my love.

Ancestors and Bagpipes

I hear distant sounds
of bagpipes
playing in my dreams.
I hear voices calling me
through lochs and
down mountain streams.
I feel the tartan plaid
scratch my naked soul
as it wraps itself
around me
and takes me back to
places of old.
My ancestors gather
around me
and greet me with a hug
and a shot of whisky
to warm me
from the biting air.
It acts like a cosy rug.
The air is crisp and clear.
I see mountains I'm ready
to roam.
I feel as if I belong here
in this place
I now call home.

Farewell to a Friend

When we lose a friend,
it's time to send
our sadness onto the breeze
and hope she feels the tears we shed,
which action fills our hearts with such
ease.

It's been many years since I last saw you,
but you were part of my life for so long.
I'm so sorry for your family.
Your beautiful notes will be missing from their song.

Farewell as you leave us
and ride the sunbeam through the sky.
It was fun to have spent some time with you.
Now it's time to say goodbye.

Friendship

To friends I might not see
or talk to for a while,
please put this little heart
in your pocket
and know it carries with it
a smile.
It doesn't matter where you live
or how far you roam,
a friend is a friend
and someone who cares;
our connection is like home.
So, if I ever leave here
and travel to far and beyond,
thank you for letting me know you.
It's been a privilege to share this bond.
So many people come and go
from our lives each day,
but there are always those who are special,
who pull up a chair and stay.
So, thank you for your friendship,
whether in person or online.
Life presents us with many hurdles,
but having friends helps to make
everything just fine.

Sunset Thoughts

As I sit on a sandy shore
and look far out to sea,
I think about life
and all that has affected me.
I see visions of times since passed.
I see dreams ahead,
of hopes and wishes I have asked.
I see faces of those who have left footprints
on my heart,
those who have come and gone,
and those with whom I never want to part.
I think about lots of time wasted
on all the wrong things,
time I can never get again,
precious moments turned into scars and stings.
As I dig my toes into the soft white sand,
I watch seabirds dive and play.
I find a beautiful shell near my hand.
As the evening draws near
and I wait for the sun to go down,
the wind gets cooler.
Into the colours of the sky I soon drown.
Orange and red feast my eyes.
People sit and stare
into the late afternoon skies.
It's been a nice day.
As I try to keep warm,
I get lost for a moment
when the day's curtains are drawn.

A Walk in a Picture Book

It's cool on the pier today.
The boats tethered to the poles
gently sway to the movement of the sea.
The fishermen are lined up,
looking hopefully at their lines
or sharing tales about the one that got away.
I love the smells that surround me,
the smell of the ocean, the scent of the seaweed,
the cooking smells from the nearby café.
They remind I am here, I am alive.
I wrap my cardigan around my shoulders;
it's a bit cooler than usual.
There's a smile from one of the crew
as he fixes ropes.
I wonder what adventures he's had.
I put my hair up in a ponytail
as it blows around my face.
A seagull hops in close to a fisherman.
"Any food mate, maaate?" it squawks.
I love the texture of the pier;
the timber has had many batterings
from the winds, the rain, and the seas,
yet here it still stands full of beautiful
character and strength.
Some of the yachts are very big and impressive;
others have had their day,
their adventures way behind them now.
As I sigh and breathe in the sea air,
I smile to myself.
It's like walking through a storybook.
I am the woman standing on the pier
in the illustration,
and the beauty of life surrounds me.

Mon Cher

When I think of you,
I become a woman,
a woman who walks
in a bubble of happiness,
a bubble that bursts
into a thousand sparkles
when she thinks of you ...
a woman who longs to feel
your breath so close
that it excites her senses ...
a woman who longs to look
into your eyes
and feel like she is swimming
in heaven ...
a woman who wears an air
of self-confidence,
knowing there is someone
who is thinking of her
lovingly.
I can't wait to see you,
mon cher.
Time is our enemy,
keeping us apart
as if it never wants us to be,
to be together,
so we can finally dissolve
into each other
and form
one perfect heart.

Our Moment

A look like no other,
like Cupid's arrow
straight to my heart.

Prolonged.

I felt my heart melt.

The noise around us
became a distant
hum
as we shared our gaze,
our hearts,
our moment.

Broken Dreams

Cobbled paths and stepping stones,
fairy floss and candy canes.
When night turns into day,
sometimes I think I am insane.

Blue skies and raincoats.
Green grass and daisy chains.
Ocean magic and cliffs like walls.
My tears are like the summer rains.

Do you see my mind in disarray,
this way, that way, so confused?
Throwing stones at glass-covered feelings,
Shatters and shards, keeps you amused.

Once I was a fairy princess
with dreams in pink and gold,
when life was to be a fairy tale
like all the stories I was told.

Storm clouds frame photos so fake.
Jeans and T-shirts sing my song.
You are sad for all you have done.
The chain we hold is not that strong.

Shed a tear from a lonely heart.
Pink castles hold no fear.
You had a chance to have fairy floss,
but you chose to have that beer.

So, as you try to be my friend,
do I suddenly seem OK?
You say you want us for forever,
but my heart has already turned away.

Windows

Open the windows of your mind.
What do you see?
What do you find?
Sandcastles on the shore.
A rotting boat
missing an oar.
Wipe the night from your eyes.
The coffee pot boils.
There are no spies.
The echoes of the past
left graffiti on your brain.
The storms bring cleansing
from unhealed pain.
Turn to face the wind.
Don't fall back.
From where you are pinned,
it pounds at your thinking.
Fresh waters swell.
You fight what is happening;
you know it so well.
Should you go or should you stay?
Should you show your
hand and play?

You drive me crazy.
In my mind,
I thought I could escape,
only to find
that when I looked out my windows,
what did I see?
You, standing there,
Looking at me.

The Rhythm of the Night

Swirls and twirls.
Notes and chords.
Lights that flash.
Guys and broads.
The sounds of a hum
as voices gel.
Dimly lit tables.
Whoops, she fell.
Music that takes
you away from the tragic,
moving your body
in spiritual magic,
swirling your arms
like fingers of fire.
The rhythm of the song
raises you higher and higher.
The thirst of the moment
is quenched with desire.
The beat of the music
only fuels our fire.
As we move in closer,
the notes drift away.
The song is over
for yet another day.

Love You

Like a river
flowing out to sea,
I know
you will always
find me,
because
no matter wherever you roam,
my heart
will always be
your home.

I can see you
beyond the clouds.
The moon has lit
a pathway
to you.
I can jump
from star to star,
over oceans
of dreams.
I know you are
there waiting
on the other side
of the moon.

Southern Chill

The soil is damp
beneath our feet
as winter closes in
and chills the air around us,
both outside and within.
The leaves are golden
and lie scattered on the ground.
The trees stand bare and naked;
they make no rustling sound.
The winds swirl around them
and strip them of their growth.
Darkness descends upon us
like a cold wet blanket draped around
us both.
The fire starts to crackle
as sparks fly off into the night.
Like fairies they light up the sky,
and dance and play as they take flight.
We sit nearby
on logs we found
as heat permeates the air.
It's nice to sit by the fire tonight—
that feeling of a warm, comfy chair.
Winter will come and go,
and for a while we'll all stay
inside.
Jumpers on and off,
and under thick coats we will hide.
Then spring will dry
beneath our feet
and summer will warm our world.
The leaves will be green
and fill the trees
like the colours of the summer flag
now proudly unfurled.

Circus tents
all in a row.
Games we played
in soft white snow.
Climbing mountains.
Signs written in the sand.
Smiling faces
and one special hand.
Love notes scribbled
with great intent,
read in haste,
understanding what is meant.
Dancing thoughts
as smiles do sparkle.
This time it's love,
unlike the last debacle.
But out to play
we do go.
Turning back—
just so you know—
I read your note
and do love you too.
Feel my heart.
To you it's true.
Blue-sky days
and summer fun,
holding your hand
'neath the summer sun.

I Am Me

I am a person,
not an age.
I have seen many things
as I've approached each stage.
My experience is vast,
as I have travelled far.
My ship has weathered many storms.
If you look closely you'll see my scar.
But that is life ...

So please respect my person
as I travel upon this earth.
If you can't respect my wrinkles,
then you can't know of my worth.
My life is full of stories
that make me who I am.
One day I'll be a memory.
Please engage me while you can.
And such is life ...

Perception

Sometimes when we try
to focus on what
we want,
it is blurred by
all that is going on
around us
or by others' perception
of our life,
which has an effect
on how we live it.

That Special Look

When you look at me
with that smile,
I know you'll be hanging around
for more than a little while.

When I see that
twinkle in your eye,
I just grin and think,
My, oh my.

When you grab my hand
in yours,
that's when I want
to lock all the doors.
When you laugh
at things I say,
it's such a great feeling
and just makes my day.

The Sad Guitar

The guitar sat there pining.
It longed to speak again.
It had been shoved into a cupboard
because its player's fingers were consumed by pain.
It once was applauded
for the music it did give,
and the joy for all who listened
gave song the right to live.
It graced many get-togethers
and travelled many miles.
It was a treasured friend of the owner that,
when played, attracted smiles.
So here it sits so lonely,
the strings rusty with despair.
I must open up the cupboard
and play a tune to show I care.

Sunrise

As the sun slowly rises
and it's the dawn of a new day,
we try to move on
from the pain of yesterday.
The day brings fresh hope,
new things to see and do,
but it can't take away your smile
or my memory of you.

Somewhere

Somewhere
there is a place
where we can
breathe
and feel the space,
where we can talk and laugh
and feel,
and where I know
your smile
is real.

Seeking You

I come from afar
and seek the place
where I can rest my head,
where I can breathe
and see beyond
the place where I was led.
I seek the comfort
of your arms;
I know they will be safe.
I seek the comfort of your soul
in which I'll find my faith.
I have travelled many miles
to reach this tender land.
I know that I am guided;
I can feel you hold my hand.
The road that lies behind me now
has vanished from my view.
I come from afar and seek the place
in which I will find you.

Beyond

Beyond the trees
there is a place
out of my reach
with infinite space.
I see a light
and feel its pull.
I spread the branches.
The air is cool.
My senses are free
and flow to the light
beyond the trees
within my sight.

Understanding Lonely

Lonely people
on lonely streets
wandering aimlessly,
no hope for treats.
Shadows searching
for owners they've lost.
Hearts broken
at such a cost.
Mirrors reflecting
a person they don't know.
Staring in wonder, one woman asks,
"Where did my time go?"
The light slowly diminishing
as tears fill her eyes.
"Don't let this be my life!"
She silently cries.

Lonely people
in quiet rooms
slowly dying
from life's sad fumes.
It's easy to say,
"Go on, open your door.
Go for a coffee
rather than stare at the floor."
It can be hard
to get out of that chair.
Lonely people
think there is no one to care.

When you are in the mountains
with nature at its best,
where peace and beauty surround you—
of that, I can attest—
can you see what lies below you
in the desert? A plane lies broken.
In pieces are many memories
and words left unspoken.
Then there is Beirut,
where a marathon was run.
For those who came across the globe,
this challenge was their fun.
But now the streets lie empty,
laughter and high fives no longer heard.
Just blood and rubble in the street.
A cruel bombing has occurred.
Can you see the Eiffel Tower
through the dark clouds over there?
The beautiful city of Paris
has had an awful scare.
The palaces and churches
in the City of Love
are so rich in history
and blessed from up above.
Paris is where so many people,
quite a few of them in their prime,
were out and about on Friday night
with their friends, enjoying a good time.
Now these people have had their lives
torn apart
as evil gunmen spilled the blood
from many an innocent heart.

The beautiful soul of this city
has been shaken
as the river Seine flows with tears
for all those taken.
It wasn't an act of nature
or an accidental blow;
it was the type of act of darkness
that we have come to fear and know.
But we can't be afraid
to look into evil's eye,
because we stand for colour and hope—
and freedom will ride high.

Please take me back to nature,
to lochs and mountains green,
where I can protect my children and theirs
from forces unforeseen.

Her eyes were filled with wonder
as she looked upon all she could
see:
the colours of the universe,
the flowers, the ocean, the bee.
Her heart was filled
with emotion.
How wonderful her world
appears.
The little smile upon her face,
her vision, and the sounds she hears.
Her life is just beginning
on this earth, which is so old in years.
I hope the colours don't fade for her
and will never be the cause of her tears.
Her youth is fresh and vibrant.
She doesn't know destruction and hate.
She looks through the eyes of innocence.
For this earth child, I hope it's not too late.

My Songbird

The songbird sang one last song
to me
as snowflakes flurried by.
The songbird's eyes swam in tears,
knowing she could no longer try.
She sang the song each day to me.
By the window, she would stand.
A beautiful song, so sweet and pure,
gifting feathers in my hand.
If I listened closely, I could hear
the words of the tune so clear:
"Wait for me. Wait. I will return.
My promise is to come for you, my dear.
Wait until all the snowflakes fall
and a blanket of white covers the ground."
If I haven't returned by then, my love,
you will no longer hear her sound.
I sent the songbird to sing to you
and to remind you every day
that I love you with all my heart
and will return to you to stay.
But as the songbird's feathers fell
and her voice became more dim,
the notes that once held a tune of love
were silenced, with just a memory
of him.

The Journey

As I stand on the bow
and look at the beautiful ocean
that lies before me,
I know I've reached the halfway mark
and there's still uncharted water
to discover.
The lands I've stopped at
along the way
have been interesting, full of colour,
and full of drama, experiences, love, and pain.
It only makes me stronger
as I glide through these waters.
The wind guides my sails.
As the currents map my path,
there will be storms to face,
waves to conquer,
and pirates wanting to steal
treasures collected along the way.
Whatever lies ahead
will be a new adventure
to enjoy, to add more scars,
and to cause me to feel more warmth
and share more stories.
The journey ahead
will take me where I need to go
until I reach that far
horizon
and see the sunset
one last time.

Life's Steps

Life carries on
in its merry little way.
I look back at photos
and remember the day
the picture was taken:
the yard, the room, the bed
and how I felt then—
the feelings of love swirling in my head.
To be an aunty
first time around,
a brand-new mum,
a grandparent—my feelings profound.
I still feel the same.
Inside nothing has changed.
Just the years on my scoreboard have,
my skin, my hair, rearranged.
My dreams are the same.
My circle of love has expanded,
friendships forever growing.
I've experienced interesting countries in which I've landed.
Still so much to learn,
more smiles and hands to hold.
The bruises and life's badges,
sunny days, and days you just feel cold.
As I look at these photos
and step back in time,
I still feel the same.
Hopefully I'll be able to add more steps
to this rhyme.

The Mastery of a Word

A word paints a picture without a visible scene.
The scene you depict is up to you.
How it is depicted is up to the reader or the listener.
So, use your colours wisely in order to depict
what you truly mean.

The ability to let a word
take you by the hand
and lead you to
a feeling,
a place,
a person's heart,
is a fortunate talent to have.

The ability to see a word
connect with other words
and take you on a journey into
another life,
another's understanding,
a classroom of learning,
is a fortunate talent to enjoy, to benefit from,
to expand your mind, to help you grow.

The ability to speak a word
on its own or woven together
with other words,
to make a statement or conversation,
can make such a difference to
someone's life,
someone's understanding.

It is a tool that we can use to construct
a gift
to share with those
both worthy and unworthy
of receiving it.

To My Friend

I know you.
I know you are sad.
What's wrong?
I can see into your heart.
Please tell me.
I am listening.
I will not turn away.
I can hear you
even though you are quiet.
What is making you cry?
I can feel your tears.
I know many have been shed.
Talk to me.
Let me help you.
My hand is here
for you to hold.
What is it?
Can I heal your sadness?
Your eyes speak to me,
but I need to
hear
your words.
I am here.

Love

A circle of unspoken connection,
a feeling like no other,
a want that can't be purchased or sold,
a moment when your heart sings
and you want the world to hear its tune.
A look that only the two of you can see,
a smile that lassoes your heart
and won't let go.
It can take but a moment to happen,
or it can grow until you realise
it's an ache when you are apart.
It's a magical tingle when your hands clasp as one.
It's the warmth of a fire
when you are joined by passion.
It's the chill of winter
when it's time to say
goodbye.

Your Smile

Your smile lifts
the veil of my reality
and takes me
to another dimension
where we are
together.

Printed in the United States
By Bookmasters